SEEING JESUS

The Father made visible

YOUTH WITH A MISSION

ZondervanPublishingHouse
Grand Rapids, Michigan
A Division of HarperCollinsPublishers

GET CONNECTED!
Living Encounters Series

Seeing Jesus
Copyright © 2000 by Youth With A Mission

Requests for information should be addressed to:

ZondervanPublishingHouse
Grand Rapids, Michigan 49530

ISBN 0-310-22707-0

All Scripture quotations, unless otherwise indicated, are taken from the *Holy Bible: New International Version*®. NIV®. Copyright © 1973, 1978, 1984 by International Bible Society. Used by permission of Zondervan Publishing House. All rights reserved.

The articles on pages 18, 26, 29, 39, 40, 42–43, 49, 55–56, 63, 67, 68, 75, 97–104 are excerpted from Youth With A Mission study notes in *The Christian Growth Study Bible*, © 1997 by The Zondervan Corporation. Study notes © 1997 by Youth With A Mission.

All rights reserved. No part of this publication may be reproduced, stored in a retrieval system, or transmitted in any form or by any means — electronic, mechanical, photocopy, recording, or any other — except for brief quotations in printed reviews, without the prior permission of the publisher.

The Living Encounters Bible study series was produced through a dynamic team process of Youth With A Mission staff members, although each guide was created by one primary author. The team consisted of: Betty Barnett, Retha Badenhorst, Maureen Menard, Ruth Perrin, Ed Sherman, Donna Jo Taylor, and Christine Terrasson. The primary author of Seeing Jesus *was Retha Badenhorst.*

Interior design by Sherri Hoffman

Printed in the United States of America

00 01 02 03 04 05 /❖ EP/ 10 9 8 7 6 5 4 3 2

Contents

Foreword		4
Introducing Living Encounters		5
Seeing Jesus: The Father Made Visible		11
SESSION ONE:	Mirror Image of the Father *John 14:1–14*	12
SESSION TWO:	The One Who Understands *Hebrews 4:12–5:4*	22
SESSION THREE:	Following in the Footsteps of Forgiveness *Luke 7:36–50*	33
SESSION FOUR:	Jesus Our Reconciler *Ephesians 2:11–18*	44
SESSION FIVE:	On to the Finish Line with Jesus *Hebrews 12:1–13*	57
SESSION SIX:	Responding to the Cross *Luke 23:32–49*	68
Leader's Notes		79
Hearing the Voice of God		97
Principles for Effective Intercession		100
Prayer Strategies for Changing Nations		102
World Map		105
Stay Connected!		106
About Youth With A Mission		107

foreword
Close Encounters with the Living God

Welcome to the Living Encounters Bible study series! We created this unique study to help sincere seekers find a deeper revelation of God. Our God loves to be pursued. He wants us to know and love him more, and there's no better way to learn of his character and his ways than through his written Word.

The Living Encounters series offers exciting new ways for you to engage Scripture and apply its truth to your life. Through this series, each participant is encouraged into living encounters with God, his Spirit, his Word, his people, and his world.

Some elements of the study are drawn from teaching methods that have been used for decades in our Discipleship Training Schools. As our students encounter God, their perspective on life changes radically. The very truth of the Scripture connects them to the global picture, to God's heart for the peoples of the world. Therefore, the more they come to know God, the more they want to make him known.

The Living Encounters series is a wonderful Bible study tool for people of various levels of spiritual maturity. Its flexible, user-friendly format appeals to people with different learning styles and cultural perspectives. And when coupled with the teaching aids found in the Christian Growth Study Bible (Zondervan), the series is a highly effective way to draw new understanding and guidance from the Scriptures.

May this series bring you a whole new appreciation of our awesome God—and set you on the pathway to many living encounters!

—Loren Cunningham,
Founder of Youth With A Mission

Introducing Living Encounters

Did you ever hear about a person you'd never met—what he said, what he looked like, what he did—and then you met him, and somehow the picture you had formed in your mind didn't fit at all? For better or worse, you were confronted with reality! An "encounter" does not mean a secondhand report about a person or a situation; it means a face-to-face meeting. In an encounter, you meet a person, and your knowledge about him or her combines with and adapts to the living reality.

This is what "Living Encounters" is all about. You have read God's Word, the Bible, but there is a gap between what it says and what you experience. You know God's Spirit is alive and well, but life would be a lot simpler if he sat down beside you and gave you advice. You like people, but sometimes loving them seems impossible. And then there's the whole world out there—so full of need and suffering that you don't know how to even begin to help.

Living Encounters are more than an analysis of Bible passages or a tool for group discussion. They are to help you *meet* and adjust your life to God's Word, God's Spirit, God's people, and God's world. They are designed to challenge you not only to grasp truth but to live it out, to connect it to your personal world and to the larger world around you. As you apply yourself to these studies, you can expect exciting changes both in your thinking and in your lifestyle.

The Living Encounters series is versatile. Each guide is divided into six sessions and can be used within a small-group discussion in a church or on a college campus. However, the series is designed so that it is just as effective for individual study.

The guides are personal. They constantly lead you to ask, "What does this mean to me and how do I apply it in my own life?" Questions reveal needs and desires of the heart and invite you to embrace the promises, assurances, exhortations, and challenges of God's Word. As you respond, the Spirit of God will be responding to you, renewing your mind and transforming you more into the likeness of Jesus Christ—the ultimate goal of all Bible study.

The Features

Each session includes the following basic features.

Opening Vignette

To draw you into the topic at hand, each session opens with a thought-provoking narrative.

Preparing Heart and Mind

These questions open your heart and focus your mind on what God wants to say to you in the passage. If you are using Living Encounters in a group setting, we strongly encourage you to include this section during the first fifteen minutes of your discussion. Please realize, however, that the entire study will probably take about an hour and fifteen minutes. If you don't have that much time, then ask your group members to reflect on these questions before you meet together, and begin your discussion with the section "Engaging the Text."

Setting the Stage

The background information found in this sidebar will help you better understand the context of the study.

Engaging the Text

This important section leads you through a Bible passage using inductive Bible study questions. The inductive method prompts you to observe, interpret, and apply the Bible passage with a variety of question styles:

- Observation questions will help you focus on what the Bible says.
- Interpretation questions will help you step into the world of the original readers to understand better what the passage meant to them.
- Application questions will help you to apply the truth to your heart and present circumstances.

Responding to God

In this section, you will receive suggestions that will help you focus your individual or group prayer time.

Punch Line

This brief sentence or verse will reinforce the theme of the session.

Taking It Further

This section is designed to be completed between studies to reinforce and further apply what you have learned. It offers a variety of suggestions for connecting what you have studied to your everyday life.

- **Connecting to Life:** a variety of activities to stimulate your personal growth and ministry to others.
- **Digging Deeper:** additional Scriptures give a deeper and broader understanding of what the Bible says about the topic of the study.
- **Meditation:** a time to reflect more deeply on a specific verse or passage.
- **Personal Expression:** creative suggestions help you to process and apply what you've learned in the session.
- **World Focus:** an encouragement to look beyond your personal realm to the needs of our world.

Additional Features

In addition to the above, the guides contain a variety of optional features. All are designed to appeal to different learning styles and gifts and to encourage deeper integration of material into all of life. It is expected that you will choose whatever features you find most useful for each session. These optional features, found in articles throughout the sessions, include:

- Gray boxed material: often these will be devotional articles relevant to the study.
- People of Impact: a snapshot of the life of a person who models the principles studied.
- People Profile: a brief description of a people group that needs to be reached with the gospel.
- Hot Topic: a discussion starter to use with other group members to stimulate deeper thinking on a difficult subject.

Leader's Notes

Leader's notes for each session are provided at the back of each study guide.

Suggestions for Individual or Group Study

Preparing Heart and Mind

1. Ask the Lord for insight, wisdom, and grace to understand the Bible passage and apply it to your own life.
2. Choose one or more of the preparation questions and take time to think about it.

Engaging the Text

1. Read and reread the assigned Bible passage. You may find it helpful to have several different translations. A good literal translation rather than a paraphrase is recommended, such as the *New International Version*, the *New American Standard Bible*, the *New Revised Standard Version*, and the *New King James Bible*. The questions in each study are based on the *New International Version*. A Bible dictionary can also serve you well for look-

Seeing Jesus: the Father Made Visible

Jack panted on up through the foothills. From time to time he recognized a certain landmark, even after so many years—a tree bent in a certain way, an unusually shaped outcrop of rock. Well, the first time had left a definite impression on him, mainly because of the bad weather! He was heading for a particular lake, famous because, on the right day with the right weather, it reflected a perfect image of the mountain range standing majestically beyond it. That first time the sky had clouded over, and when at last he'd reached the shore of the lake, its surface was choppy and broken, the peaks only glimpsed in patches through cloud and mist. But today... "Please God!" whispered Jack.

Today, suddenly, there it was: perfect. The glasslike lake lay serenely still. The mountains towered across the skyline, and perfectly, completely, they also lay before him on the water's surface. Every peak and hollow of the mountains, every twig and branch of the trees standing along the shore, and, close to his feet, the exact representation of one feathery cloud floating high in the blue heavens. Jack sighed with utter contentment. He'd seen the perfect image.

And so it is with Jesus. Christians reflect God to us sporadically, depending on the "weather" of their lives. Some do reflect him consistently, but even the really godly ones give us a somewhat cloudy or broken picture. Not Jesus. He represents our Father, the Almighty God, perfectly, consistently, always. As the lake reflected every crag, every rock, every tree, so he reflects every aspect of God's character: his wisdom, his mercy, his justice, his ways.

Some of us have misunderstood the character of God and unknowingly distorted our picture of him. If you want a radical adjustment of your concept of the Father, a deeper understanding of his love and care for you, and a greater passion for Jesus, the one who reflects him perfectly...

...then this study is for you!

session ONE

Mirror Image of the Father
John 14:1–14

When Mary's parents came to faith in Jesus Christ, their lives changed dramatically. But their headstrong teenager wasn't interested in changing. Mary was looking for fulfillment through various means, far from her parents' wishes. After years of failed relationships, she was still searching. One day, having just discovered that she was pregnant by her latest boyfriend, she got the stunning news that her dad was dying after a heart attack.

"God must be punishing me for getting pregnant!" she burst out to a Christian acquaintance. "Why else would he take away a good man like my dad?" "But Mary, God is not like that!" her friend responded. As she explained further, Mary, in tears, understood for the first time that while God was grieved by the sin in her life, he loved her and her baby dearly. And he was reaching out to help her through the difficult times she faced.

> **The Son is ... the exact representation of his being.**
> —— **HEBREWS 1:3**

In the book *The Tutor's First Love* by George MacDonald, one of the characters says: "Don't measure God's mind by your own!" Let's face it, so often we do. We weigh God by our own standards of love, justice, fairness, and mercy. Our image of him has been woven together from scraps of philosophy and science, images from the entertainment world, experiences in our family, and other areas of life. Most of the time we have developed an image of God that is distorted and vague. We don't let God speak for himself. Our heavenly Father longs to be known for who he really is. In this study we will look at Jesus as the mirror image of God the Father. As we do so, invite the Holy Spirit to remold your understanding of God.

PREPARING HEART AND MIND

- Imagine looking down onto the surface of a windblown river. What do you see? Now imagine looking facedown into a glassy pond. What's the difference?

  Ripples - distorted face - Clearer image of self -

- What is your definition of a friend?

  someone you can trust & count on

- How much of a friend is God to you? Can you imagine sitting down to a cup of coffee with him?

  God is my best FRIEND - coFFEE? I don't know - I can imagine God with a slight grin looking at me in wonderment - saying Relax & don't take everything so serious -

SESSION ONE: Mirror Image of the Father

engaging the text

setting the stage

- It is the evening of the Passover meal and Jesus is talking to his disciples in the upper room.
- The disciples have been with Jesus for about three years.
- During the previous weeks, Jesus has repeatedly told them that he is going to die.
- This is an evening filled with emotion. The disciples are feeling confusion, fear, and grief.
- Jesus knows that later that same night he will be betrayed and arrested. This passage is part of his final instructions to his disciples. He understands their confusion and tries to comfort them.

1. When you think of God, what kind of a picture comes to your mind? Think of descriptive words that capture what you see.

   Large —
   beautiful —
   There are no words —

2. What kind of a picture comes to mind when you think of Jesus?

   Handsome —
   soft —
   Calm
   Peacefilled
   understanding
   Patient
   humor filled (Sense of humor)

Read John 14:1–14

3. How many times does Jesus refer to the Father in these verses?

14

What do you think he is trying to emphasize about the Father?

To trust in Him —

The Principle of Repetition

Repetition is one of the best ways of teaching to get a point across more fully. We often find this principle in the Bible. When studying the Scriptures, taking note of repetition may give you new insights. For example, Genesis 1 often repeats the phrase "and God saw that it was good." And in Leviticus, the word "holy" is repeated about eighty-nine times in only twenty-seven chapters, showing us that the focus is not on these "tedious" laws but on the fact that God is holy and wants us to lead holy lives.

4. Jesus is drawing several parallels between himself and the Father (vv. 1, 6–11). What are they?

   That God & Jesus are one & the same —

   To trust

5. How might these parallels be reassuring to the disciples in their troubled state? (See Setting the Stage.)

6. Is one or more of these parallels also reassuring to you in your present walk with God? Explain.

7. Identify aspects of Jesus' character that are demonstrated in this passage (see also Setting the Stage). Note both *what* he says and *how* he says it.

8. In verse 4, Jesus assures the disciples that they know the way to the place where he is going, but Thomas doesn't seem to have a clue what Jesus is talking about. What do you think is the reason for this gap in communication?

9. What more do we discover about Jesus in his response to Thomas?

10. In verse 8, Philip expresses a desire to see the Father. What, according to Jesus, is Philip failing to grasp?

Only Through Him!

"Jesus answered, 'I am the way and the truth and the life. No one comes to the Father except through me'" (John 14:6).

11. Both Thomas and Philip are looking for answers outside of Jesus—for their comfort, direction, and security—but Jesus points them back to himself. Describe a time when you felt like Thomas or Philip, searching for answers outside of Jesus.

Face-to-Face

"The Word became flesh and made his dwelling among us. We have seen his glory, the glory of the One and Only, who came from the Father, full of grace and truth" (John 1:14).

Millions of people today communicate with each other via electronic mail. Some say they prefer to build relationships this way—perhaps because there is relatively little risk involved. We also may feel freer to express ourselves when facing a computer monitor or a piece of paper than we do when talking with someone.

In spite of these benefits, we intuitively understand that we don't really know a person until we have met them in person. Many people have felt that they had found love with a pen pal or an acquaintance on the Internet, only to be bitterly disappointed when they met in person.

God gave us his law through Moses and described himself through Abraham, David, and other prophets. But those laws and descriptions would never be enough to enable us to say that we really know who God is.

Having given his Word, God showed just how committed he is by becoming one of us. Thanks be to God that Jesus became a human being! Now we need not be satisfied with laws and written descriptions of God in heaven. He is incarnate. The Word has become flesh and dwells among us!

As you consider your relationship with the Lord, is he a friend with whom you talk and share? He wants that kind of deeply personal relationship with you.

12. Think back to your response to Question 2. In what ways has your perspective of Jesus as God changed? How might you respond differently to Jesus now?

13. The Father is like Jesus, that is, they think the same, act the same, love, care, and forgive in the same manner. Think back to your response to Question 1. As you consider what you have learned in this study, how might the way you now respond and relate to God the Father change?

[Handwritten at top:] That God was this GIANT UP IN the SKY that Judged & punished when we were "Bad"
I didn't know God as a kind Loving God —

RESPONDING TO GOD

Pray for a greater understanding of who God the Father and Jesus really are. Ask God to correct the distorted image you might have of the Father and of Jesus.

JESUS =
accessible,
knowable,
visible
= the Father

ing up any unfamiliar words, people, places, or theological concepts. Commentaries, while having great value, are not part of this kind of study, which uses the inductive method.
2. The questions are designed to help you make observations, draw conclusions, and apply God's truth to your life. Write your answers in the space provided. Recording your observations and conclusions is an important step in any study process. It encourages you to think through your answers thoroughly, thus furthering the learning process.
3. Note the optional elements offered in the sidebars. These are designed to encourage greater understanding of the passage being studied.
4. Be aware of the continuous presence of the Lord throughout the process. You may want to stop and pray in the midst of your study. Be sure to end your study with a time of waiting, listening, and responding to the Lord in prayer.
5. Be willing to participate in the discussion. The leader of the group will not be lecturing; rather, he or she will be encouraging the members of the group to discuss what they have learned from the passage. The leader will be asking the questions that are found in this guide. Plan to share what God has taught you in your individual study time.
6. Stick to the passage being studied. Your answers should be based on the verses which are the focus of the discussion and not on outside authorities such as commentators or speakers (or the commentary notes in your study Bible!).
7. Be sensitive to other members of the group. Listen attentively when they share. You can learn a lot from their insights! Stick with the topic—when you have insights on a different subject, keep it for another time so the group is not distracted from the focus of the study.
8. Be careful not to dominate the discussion. We are sometimes so eager to share that we leave too little opportunity for others to contribute. By all means participate, but allow others to do so as well.

9. Expect the Holy Spirit to teach you both through the passage and through other members of the group. Everyone has a unique perspective that can broaden your own understanding. Pray that you will have an enjoyable and profitable time together.
10. The "Responding to God" section is the place where you pray about the topics you have studied. At this time you will invite the Holy Spirit to work these truths further into each of your lives. Be careful not to overlook this essential aspect of your time together.

Taking It Further

1. Identify other questions that arise through the study so that you can pursue them later.
2. Choose one or more of the activities to help you apply the principles in your life. These are optional activities to be done on your own after the Bible study session.

Leader's Notes

If you are the discussion leader or simply want further information, you will find additional suggestions and ideas for each session in the Leader's Notes in the back of this guide.

taking it further
Suggestions for application

DIGGING DEEPER

For further study on the oneness of God the Father and Jesus, see:

John 1:1–5; 10–14; Hebrews 1:1–4.

Connecting to Life

Write down your perceptions and images of God the Father that you realize have been distorted. Ask Jesus to go with you to the Father with your thoughts and views. Spend time in prayer, committing it all to him. Expect a change of view!

Meditation

Read Colossians 1:15–20 four or five times in one sitting. Then answer the following questions:
- Who are the two main characters in this passage?
- What parallel is Paul drawing between God and Jesus?
- Make a list of all the things that Paul says about Jesus.

In light of what you have understood, write out a prayer of thanksgiving or a request to God.

[handwritten: CHRIST God / The g Rescue]

WORLD FOCUS

God's desire is for all peoples to come to know him as a loving, personal Father who is always accessible to all who call on his name. Think of a people group or nation with which you are familiar and which is not known as "Christian." Using the "Principles for Effective Intercession" on pages 100–101, pray for these people.

SESSION ONE: Mirror Image of the Father

session two

The One Who Understands
Hebrews 4:12–5:4

She knew Mom would say no, so eight-year-old Molly didn't even ask. Mom was next door, and the cookie jar containing the peanut butter balls was on top of the fridge. Peanut butter balls were Molly's favorite! Climbing on a chair and retrieving the jar was a simple matter. Eating one or two balls was a simple matter too. Eating three or four was no problem. Nine, ten . . .

Mom knew something was amiss at dinnertime when Molly called downstairs that she didn't want to eat. She found Molly crouched in the bathroom, clutching her middle and tearfully ready to confess what she'd done. Surprisingly, Mom didn't seem shocked. She got the stomach medicine, helped Molly to bed, and brought her a drink. "Well, it's no dessert for you for a week," said Mom gently, "but I guess you're already sorry you disobeyed."

"I am, Mom! But why aren't you mad at me? You're being so nice!"

Mom laughed. "I do understand, you know. I was a little girl once. Have I ever told you why I don't like tomatoes? I once loved them. When I was about your age, I ate a whole row of green tomatoes my mother was ripening on the windowsill. Was I ever sick! I know just how you feel right now."

In a small way Molly's story reflects what we can experience with Jesus. Because he became a man and walked through life on this earth, Jesus understands how we feel. In the book of Hebrews, we read that although he never sinned, he knows only too well what temptation is like. In fact, nothing is hidden from him. In this study, we will look at what it means to have such an understanding "high priest" as Jesus, who reflects the immense patience and understanding of the Father.

> **His understanding no one can fathom.**
>
> —Isaiah 40:28

PREPARING HEART AND MIND

- Imagine having all your thoughts and motives projected on a screen for everybody to see. How would you feel?

    embarased & ashamed

- Would you feel the same if it was only God who sees the screen? Why?

    Yes & No – God already sees & knows what I think, feel & do.

engaging the text

setting the stage

- The book of Hebrews is written by an unknown Jewish author to Jewish Christians undergoing persecution because of their faith.

- In Hebrews 4 and 5, Jesus is presented as the Christians' "high priest." The role of the high priest in the Old Testament is:

  - To present sacrifices and offerings for his own sins (Leviticus 4:3) and for the sins of the people (Leviticus 5:5; 6:6–7; 16:15–17).

  - To consult God regarding matters affecting the nation and inform the people of what God says.

Read Hebrews 4:12–5:4

1. What do you think is the key message in this passage?

   How does this make you feel?

2. In verses 14–16, the author calls on us to do two things and also gives reasons why we should do them. Describe these.

- Things we are to do:

  (A) never stop trusting him
  (B) come to Him

- Why we are to do them:

  to recieve His mercy & Grace

In what ways might this change your perspective on approaching God? Why?

3. Think of an area of temptation that you have struggled with. If someone said to you, "Hey, I've been there! There is a way out; let me show you," how would this affect you or your actions?

Unique, Royal—But One of Us

No one was ever born like Jesus. He is the only baby to be born of a human mother but without a human father.

Jesus' family tree is found in Matthew 1—a passage easy to skip over, but so significant because it tells us that God placed Jesus in David's royal family. Luke 3 traces Mary's family tree. She also descended from King David. Keeping his divine nature as the eternal God, Jesus took on humanity through his mother. Jesus was fully God, and he was fully man.

The fact that God came down to earth in the form of a tiny baby is hard to comprehend. The truth that the limitless love and life of the Ruler of the universe compressed down into a span of little humanity is the central reality of the Bible record: "The Word became flesh and made his dwelling among us" (John 1:14). Jesus, as one of us, identified with all the realities of life.

When sharing your faith with followers of other religions, it is important to note that what makes Christianity unique is that God loved us so much that he became a person and lived among us.

4. "Jesus sympathizes with your weaknesses and understands your struggles perfectly." In what ways might a revelation of this truth make a difference (or bring hope) in your situation?

That we are not alone —

5. In chapter 4, Jesus is compared to a high priest. According to 5:1–4, what are the criteria for becoming a high priest in the Old Testament, his functions and abilities?

Criteria	Functions	Abilities

6. How does Jesus "measure up" to each of these points?

Hot topic

It seems almost blasphemous to think that Jesus could have been tempted by sins that can eventually result in shocking activities, such as torturing and killing, prostitution, drug dealing, Satan worship, or sexual sins. Yet this is exactly what Hebrews 4:15 states. We all face severe temptations at times, and Jesus "was tempted in every way, just as we are—yet was without sin." There are people who desperately need to know that there is a high priest who understands their need, temptation, and confusion, and who can save them, no matter how deep they have fallen. But not everyone considers them worth being helped, or able to be saved.

Who does the world find impossible to forgive? How should we, as God's ambassadors, respond to these people?

7. Think of a time when you did something wrong and had to "face the music." How did you approach the person who would likely punish you? Explain why.

Troll incident
So much guilt.

In your experience, are Christians more or less judgmental than non-Christians? Explain.

It depends on who it is - most "TRUE" CHRISTIANS ARE NOT - The ones who call themselves CHRISTIANS & ARE EXTREME ARE judgemental -

SESSION TWO: The One Who Understands

8. In 4:16, why do you think the image is of a "throne" of grace and not an altar or something else?

Because God is our King - King sits on a throne & watches over us -

Bearing Our Weaknesses

As Jesus understands us, he wants us also to be understanding of one another. Sometimes the smallest things can be the biggest irritants in our personal relationships. Annoying habits, uncorrected faults, tiresome expressions, and inconsiderate ways of doing things often rub us the wrong way and shake our unity as believers.

The Lord wants us not just to tolerate one another, but to bear lovingly and gently with one another, allowing him to do the work of correction. The writer of Hebrews implies two reasons why many of us find this difficult. One is a lack of compassion and identification with others. The other is our unwillingness to face our own weaknesses, which are as irritating to others as theirs are to us.

Forbearance does not mean that we should ignore one another's faults. Yet it is the character trait that gives us patience and gentleness to wait for the appropriate time to approach the matter in a helpful way.

In what ways are you lacking forbearance and grace toward others? How can you change? Ask God to remind you every time you respond to another without forbearance and grace.

9. What keeps people from approaching this throne of grace?

   FEAR -

10. What might help you to approach this throne more readily when you need to?

    KNOWING God -

11. Do you have an area of struggle in which you would be helped by coming to this throne of grace? Explain.

    YES - the male trust issue.

Responding to God

Take time to thank Jesus that he understands you and your weaknesses and he loves you anyway. Thank him also for reflecting the understanding and love that God the Father has toward us. Ask him to help you do the same for other people.

Jesus—where understanding and grace encounter our weaknesses.

taking it further
Suggestions for application

DIGGING DEEPER

For additional study about the God who understands us perfectly, read these verses in the following order:

Hebrews 2:17–18;
Exodus 34:6;
Psalm 103:13–14;
147:5; Job 12:13.

Personal Expression

Paint a picture or create a sculpture in clay or other material depicting yourself at God's throne of grace. Let it show by posture or expression what you desire your attitude to be.

WORLD FOCUS

"For we do not have a high priest who is unable to sympathize with our weaknesses" (Hebrews 4:15). Think of a person and/or group of people in the world news who really need to *know* that Jesus understands and can identify with their struggles and circumstances. Refer to "Principles for Effective Intercession" on pages 100–101 and pray for them. "Prayer Strategies for Changing Nations" on pages 102–4 could also be very helpful.

Connecting to Life

Think of someone you know who is struggling with something that you find difficult to identify with. Ask God to show you how he sees this person and what you might do to support him or her. For instance, you could give a gift or send a card to say, "You are not alone."

Christina w/ her husband & money issues - I don't get it -

Following in the Footsteps of Forgiveness
Luke 7:36–50

session **three**

The late Corrie ten Boom learned a lot about forgiveness as a Dutch woman in the time of the Nazi occupation of her country, and later she traveled and taught about it for many years. However, she was speaking once in a German city when a former Nazi came up to the platform to ask for her forgiveness. She instantly recognized him as a guard from the German concentration camp where she had been imprisoned during World War II.

Suddenly, old feelings of anger, hurt, and vengeance swelled within her. "Lord, I can't forgive him," she cried inside. He and the others had caused so much suffering, and it was under their cruelty that Corrie's sister had died. Yet Jesus Christ had given his life for this man also. The still small voice of the Lord prompted her, "Forgive him for my sake."

> "Forgive us our debts, as we also have forgiven our debtors."
>
> — **matthew 6:12**

She decided to do so, though she felt nothing, no warmth, no kindness. She extended her hand and the moment their hands clasped, she felt a rush of forgiveness flow through her. The *feeling* of forgiveness followed the *act* of her will.

When Jesus gave his life for us, he reflected profoundly our heavenly Father's longing to remove the barriers of sin and have fellowship with us. As we look at this study, ask the Holy Spirit to help you understand the true meaning of forgiveness so that you can grasp God's perspective and start to live it out as Jesus does.

PREPARING HEART AND MIND

- How easy do you find it to:

    accept forgiveness?

    I ACCEPT IT, but when IT comes to MURDER & Terrible CRimes - IT is very difficult TO UNDERSTAND. I KOW God forgives ALL, but IT doesn't make SENSE to me. sometimes -

    forgive yourself?

    Very difficult for me - I don't feel deserving -

    forgive others?

    EASIER than forgiving self.

- Why? IT has always been easier for me to forgive others ACTIONS over my own - I guess I feel THAT I should Know better.

engaging the text

Setting the Stage

- Hospitality is of utmost importance in biblical times. Withholding customary acts of hospitality would be a great insult.

- *Kissing the feet:* This is a common practice among the Jews of this time. It is a mark of affection and reverence and also practiced by those who have an important request to present.

- *Washing the feet:* In hot, dry climates where sandals are worn, frequent foot washing becomes a necessity for comfort and health. It is as much a part of hospitality for a host to see that his guests' feet are washed as it is to provide them with food.

- *Anointing guests:* This is part of the ceremonies for the coronation of kings and the installation of the high priest, but is also an act of courtesy and hospitality toward a guest.

- *Kiss of greeting:* The kiss on the cheek as a mark of respect or an act of greeting is a custom in the East.

Read Luke 7:36–50

1. There are several things Simon fails to do in greeting Jesus (see Setting the Stage). What is the significance of this failure?

2. As a Pharisee, Simon would know the Jewish laws and customs extremely well. What does his neglect of Jesus tell us about him?

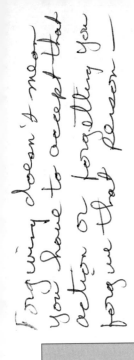

Forgiving doesn't mean you have to accept that action or forgetting, you forgive that person!

3. Imagine being at the feast. If you were the one to whom normal hospitality was so obviously denied, how would you feel and respond?

4. Consider how Jesus might feel. In contrast, how does he respond, according to the text?

Forgiveness Is Not Easy!

When someone breaks your favorite pen, it is a comparatively simple choice to forgive. But when someone breaks your heart, it's quite another story! The pain involved is so great that "making choices" just isn't enough. This is when you need Jesus and his grace. Peter asked Jesus how many times he should forgive his brother. What was Jesus' response? Seventy-seven times (Matthew 18:21–22)!

Is it possible that Jesus means this to be true for you too, in your situation? That would mean that you might have to forgive and forgive again . . . and again . . . and again . . . for the very same thing!

And will the pain go away once you have forgiven? Yes—eventually! Experiencing pain doesn't mean that you haven't forgiven. It just means that you need to forgive again. And Jesus, who knows all about a broken heart, will be right there with more grace and mercy than you will ever need.

5. Why does Jesus wait until later to confront Simon?

What does this tell us about Jesus' character?

6. Try to put yourself in Simon's shoes (or sandals!) when Jesus addresses him. What do you think he hears and feels when Jesus tells the parable (vv. 41–43)?

Now try to put yourself in the woman's shoes as she listens to the same parable. What do you think she hears and feels?

Hot topic

Simon is guilty of the sin of lips that will not kiss, hands that refuse to wash Jesus' feet, neglect of perfume to be poured out. The woman may be guilty of a heart that has been sinful, but Simon is guilty of a heart that is hard!

A sinful heart or a (hard heart) which is worse?

7. What do you think Jesus means when he says, "But he who has been forgiven little loves little" (v. 47)?

8. "The more you're aware of your own need for forgiveness, the more you're willing to forgive others." Do you agree or disagree with this statement? Explain why.

9. In Matthew 6:14–15, Jesus says: "For if you forgive men when they sin against you, your heavenly Father will also forgive you. But if you do not forgive men their sins, your Father will not forgive your sins." On the basis of what Jesus says, consider the following statement: "Forgiveness should be a lifestyle, not just an occasional event." Does this strengthen or weaken you own opinion of forgiveness? Explain why.

A Time for Restoration

Read 2 Chronicles 28:1–5; 29:1–2.

The horrible reign of King Ahaz left deep scars on his kingdom and on his son Hezekiah. With a father like that, it's easy to grow bitter. But bitterness perpetuates the legacy of sin and retards spiritual growth. Because Hezekiah trusted God as his Father, he did not succumb to this bitterness. He went on to become one of Judah's greatest and most righteous kings.

Like Hezekiah, many people have grown up in a destructive environment. One young woman, Marcy, endured years of her father's verbal and physical abuse. This devastating experience robbed her of hope and value. But God did not abandon her. Despite these horrible circumstances, he wanted to give her a fresh start. The process of restoration began when she honestly acknowledged her pain and asked God to help her forgive her dad.

One of the key roles of the Holy Spirit is to reveal the true Father to us, empowering us to let go of bitterness and to take hold of his love and acceptance.

Has life left you bruised? Don't settle for bitterness. Ask God to lead you in forgiveness and in steps of restoration.

Responding to God

Ask God to soften your heart in the areas where it is still hard and unforgiving. Ask him to help you to follow in the footsteps of Jesus and forgive those who have hurt or insulted you.

forgiveness: you can't afford to live without it!

taking it further
Suggestions for application

DIGGING DEEPER

For further study on God's abundant forgiveness toward us and our own responsibility to forgive others, see:

Numbers 14:19; Nehemiah 9:17; Matthew 18:32–33; Mark 2:10; 11:25; Luke 11:4; 23:34; Colossians 3:13; 1 John 1:9.

Personal Expression

What does forgiveness look like to you? Create a picture, a card, or an object that demonstrates either God's forgiveness toward you or your forgiveness toward someone who has hurt you. Keep it in a prominent place as a reminder to you of the forgiveness you have received and/or extended.

WORLD FOCUS

The Dai of China and Thailand are a people group who desperately need to know this God who is ready to show them his forgiveness and cleanse them through Jesus Christ. Read about the Dai on the next two pages and take time to pray for them. "Prayer Strategies for Changing Nations" (pages 102–4) could be helpful as you do so.

PEOPLE PROFILE

the Dai—Only the Living Water Will Truly Cleanse Them

Location: China, Thailand. Population: 1 million. Religion: 80% Buddhist.

Although the sun had not yet risen, the village resounded to the barks of dogs and the cries of children. His mother had already bathed and dressed young Sawat when Ailang plunged himself under the water. Like all the other Dai people, Ailang's family was getting ready to attend the *danfo* service at the village Buddhist temple.

Ailang was allowed to carry the family offerings of money, rice, papayas, and flowers. As his family offered incense, Ailang presented their offerings to the gilded statue of Buddha. Monks were chanting Buddhist scriptures, and devoted Dai lips silently murmured prayers. The first shafts of light for the New Year pierced the incense clouds hanging in the temple.

Small children let out squeals of delight as Buddha's statue glowed in the sunlight. Several of the men moved forward, hoisted the statue onto strong bamboo poles, and carried it into the courtyard. This was the signal the women had been waiting for. Along with the other village women, Mi Ailang showered Buddha with water. The Water Sprinkling Festival had begun.

Before Mi Ailang could refill her basin, Ailang and Sawat, aided by their father, tossed water over their mother. Water drenched the courtyard as Dai families sprinkled water over anyone within range. Water, laughter, and joy mark the beginning of every Dai New Year. The Dai believe that water washes away the sins of the last year and carries with it any potential disasters from the year to come. The Water Sprinkling Festival lasts several days with everyone getting drenched repeatedly. Mi Ailang saw to it that her children were sprinkled often and thoroughly; she wanted to ensure that last year's sins wouldn't follow Ailang and Sawat into the new year.

Pray that:
- Dai families would come into relationship with the great high priest, Jesus Christ (Hebrews 4:14; 7:24).
- The Dai would understand they can sprinkle their bodies clean but not their hearts.
- Hebrews 10:19–22 would be proclaimed over the Dai people.
- Entire Dai families would have the opportunity to hear about the One who alone can offer them living water (John 4:14; 7:38).
- The Dai would come to know that Jesus paid the price for complete forgiveness for all their sins and that they too would reflect to one another the forgiving heart of God.

Jesus Our Reconciler
Ephesians 2:11–18

session four

Jane was just a toddler when her mother put her up for adoption. The hurt and bitterness of rejection dominated her life for two decades. When she committed her life to God and attended a discipleship training school, the healing began. But the greatest surprise of her life was in store for her.

In a "coincidence" that only God could arrange, she discovered that the one older woman in her class was her birth mother—who had also committed her life to Jesus Christ! The God of love had arranged their reunion and their reconciliation!

What if Jane and her mother had met unexpectedly like this, but without knowing the Lord? Surely the hurt and bitterness of years would have made it extremely difficult, if not impossible, for them to come close to a normal relationship. But the Spirit of God was now living in both of them, and they experienced the truth that, by the power of Christ, dividing walls can be broken down and two parties can be reconciled in peace.

> **Through him [God was pleased] to reconcile to himself all things.**
>
> —**Colossians 1:20**

In Paul's time, the young church often experienced conflict between believers of Jewish and Gentile background. In his letter to the Ephesians, he points out the unique power of Jesus to join such diverse groups of people into one, united body. As we look at what Paul writes, pray that you will grow in your understanding of what Jesus our reconciler has done for us.

Preparing Heart and Mind

- How would you describe peace?

- How would you describe reconciliation?

- What connection is there between peace and reconciliation?

engaging the text

setting the stage

- Racial strife and tension are rampant between Jews and Gentiles (all non-Jews) in the early church.

- Jews consider themselves superior to Gentiles. However, Gentiles have conquered and enslaved the Jews.

- In the minds of many Jewish Christians, it is impossible to have fellowship with Gentile Christians who do not follow Jewish food and circumcision laws.

- Paul has paid a high price to help people understand that Jesus came to bring peace to troubled hearts and communities—both Jewish and Gentile—and to break down dividing walls between people.

Read Ephesians 2:11–18

1. "Peace is merely the absence of conflict." Do you agree or disagree? Why?

2. Paul mentions two groups of people, Gentile believers ("you") and Jews ("them"). How does he describe each of them? Note the contrasts between them.

Verse	Group 1: "You"	Group 2: "Them"

Figures of Speech

In referring to the two groups as "uncircumcised" and "the circumcision," Paul is using a figure of speech. He is employing one term to represent another in order to make a point. By using these particular terms, Paul is in effect saying, "This is not just who you are, but it is the label representing everything that divides you."

Different kinds of figures of speech are scattered throughout the Bible. Look for them as you study the Scriptures.

3. In verse 14, Paul refers to a "barrier" or "dividing wall" that separates the Jews and Gentiles. What barriers or dividing walls can you identify in the church today? Consider external as well as internal barriers.

4. How do these kinds of barriers destroy peace within the church and society?

5. In what ways do barriers cause problems in your own relationships?

6. In verses 13–16, Paul emphasizes that "in Christ" reconciliation is possible for the Jew and Gentile groups. What did Jesus do to reconcile the groups both to the Father and to one another?

Don't Worry about the Carpet

Read Psalm 133.

Christians fight over such petty things at times. Issues like what color of carpet to put in the church sanctuary, what type of music to use in worship services, or how to run church social events have split entire congregations. Other times, churches and relationships break apart over more substantial issues of doctrine or leadership. But the net effect is still the same—people are wounded and the church loses out on God's blessing.

Psalm 133 gives us two wonderful pictures of how good it is when believers live in unity. Oil represents God's Spirit. When it pours down Aaron's whole body, it symbolizes how God's love drenches those who are totally devoted to him. Likewise, dew falling on the mountains is an image of God's promise to nourish the land and bring fruitfulness to his people.

Where there is disunity and conflict, Jesus made it possible to find a place of reconciliation. Even when we're living in unity, there's still room for us to have different opinions. Paul pointed out that Jesus reconciled Jew and Gentile to become "one new man." So can he enable us to build our lives together on the essentials of our faith (1 Corinthians 15:1–5) while allowing the freedom for diversity and even for disagreement on some nonessential issues. We just have to be willing to lay down our own preferences so that Jesus Christ is glorified. As we remain devoted to him and to one another, he will make us a holy, unselfish people—among whom he delights to dwell.

How do these thoughts shed light on any unresolved conflicts or disagreements you have? Will you make reconciliation and unity a high priority? Are there some attitudes or actions you need to change?

Why did this make reconciliation possible?

7. In verse 14, Paul says that Jesus "is our peace." Explain how this is true in your life.

8. "If we are not reconciled to God, there is no way that we will ever be reconciled to one another." Do you agree or disagree with this statement? Explain why.

Peace

A definition for peace: The presence and experience of healthy relationships.

9. Jesus has brought reconciliation between the two groups in order to "create in himself one new man out of the two" (vv. 14–16). In your own words, explain what this means. Be practical!

10. Both Jew and Gentile need to be reconciled to God (v. 16), and what is true for people in Paul's time is still true for us today. What things still separate people from God today? (Do any of these affect you?)

11. Jesus' work of reconciliation cost him a tremendous price. Think of a situation where you need to see reconciliation take place between you and another person or a particular group. What would it cost you to do something about it?

12. Verse 17 says that Jesus "preached peace," yet in the gospels there is very little record of Jesus mentioning peace. What do you think Paul means?

13. As a follower of Jesus, how can you "preach" peace? (Consider how you can help toward reconciling people with God or with one another.)

Peacemakers

"Blessed are the peacemakers, for they will be called sons of God" (Matthew 5:9).

Responding to God

Spend time thanking the Father for the free access that you have to him. Thank Jesus for making this possible.

> **Peace cost Jesus his life. Have you taken hold of it?**

SESSION FOUR: Jesus Our Reconciler

taking it further
Suggestions for application

DIGGING DEEPER

For further study on the peace and reconciliation that Jesus provides for us, see:

Romans 5:1; Colossians 1:19–20; 3:15; 1 Timothy 2:5–6.

WORLD FOCUS

Read about the Turkana people group on page 55. Using "Principles for Effective Intercession" on pages 100–101, pray for these people.

Connecting to Life

Think again of how you answered Question 11. Identify one or more relationships in your life where you still need to see reconciliation take place. This could be a group, or even a nationality or race, not just individuals. Ask God to show you what practical and prayerful steps you can take to move toward reconciliation. Take action.

Meditation

Although there is not much record of what Jesus said on the subject of peace, read through the following verses. Stop after each one and ask yourself the question, "In what way does this passage apply to me in my present circumstances?"

- Matthew 10:13 (also Luke 10:5–6)
- Matthew 10:34 (also Luke 12:51)
- Mark 9:50
- John 14:27
- John 16:33

PEOPLE PROFILE

the turkana—desperate for a downpour of heavenly blessing

Location: Kenya. Population: 317,000. Religion: 80% Animist, 20% Christian.

Drought had ravaged the grasslands for so long that few of the Turkana children knew what it was to run and splash in the rain. Ebei tugged at Lomoria's arm and said, "Tell it again, tell it again!" The story of the rainmaking ceremony with the crack of thunder as the rain fell in heavy warm splotches was Ebei's favorite. Lomoria began the story once again, and Ebei and the other children sat at his feet in hushed suspense. When the story was over, Ebei asked Lomoria why the rain refused to come anymore, but before he could answer, Ebei's older brother summoned him to help with the family chores.

Why do the rains fail us? Lomoria thought. This was the question that had troubled his people for too long. The tribal elders believed that a broken taboo had caused the rains to fail and their cattle to die; they believed there was a powerful curse on the land.

Turkana had always lived at peace with the neighboring Ngijie tribe. The two tribes raided each other's cattle, but it was unthinkable to harm or kill a Ngijie. Yet the unthinkable had happened. Young warriors, carried away by the excitement of the cattle raid, had killed and wounded many Ngijie. Since that time the rains had failed, the grasses had withered, and Turkana cattle had died. The warriors had brought a curse on the Turkana lands. Bloodguilt hung over Lomoria's people.

In 2 Samuel 21, bloodguilt hung over David's people, the tribes of Israel. In his zeal, Saul had broken a covenant with the Gibeonites by killing them. The land was cursed with famine

SESSION FOUR: Jesus Our Reconciler

until David sought the Lord on how to deal with it and restore rain to the land. Who will lead the Turkana to seek the Lord? Who will show them how they can be reconciled—tribe to tribe? Who will tell them that in Jesus Christ every curse is broken?

Pray that:
- Turkana children would receive a double blessing: the chance to play in the rain and to hear the good news that Jesus has broken the curse over mankind.
- Turkana elders would seek God as David did, finding reconciliation of mankind to God, as well as reconciliation between tribes.
- Those Turkana elders who hear Biblical stories, such as the one in 2 Samuel 21, would seek God's help for their land and their own people.

On to the Finish Line with Jesus
Hebrews 12:1–13

session
five

Beth and her husband had a good relationship. They worked in the same company, enjoyed similar pastimes, and attended church regularly. As the years went by, the only thing that marred their happiness was their inability to have children. It was terribly disappointing, but it also meant they could take lots of vacations. Then one day Beth's secure world exploded. Her loving husband got involved with another woman, who was now expecting his baby! He eventually divorced Beth to marry the mother of his child.

A crushing darkness engulfed Beth. All she could do was cling to God, who, she knew, was somehow with her in her grief. And slowly, as she cried out to Jesus, peace settled in her heart. What she had read in the Bible began to take on a reality she hadn't known before. With the Lord's strength, she even found the ability to forgive her husband and his new wife.

> **He who began a good work in you will carry it on to completion.**
>
> — **Philippians 1:6**

Though Beth's future looked dark, she refused to give in. Jesus really was light to her as she looked ahead. She dedicated her life to God in a deeper way than ever before and sensed that he had something more for her. Eventually she attended a training program for missionaries and went to one of the poorest countries in Africa to share the good news of the gospel. Beth would never have chosen the events that led her to this new life, but what joy she found in it! So many Africans around her were suffering, and she could share with them about the strength and grace that Jesus gives to endure hardship and persevere to the finish line with him!

PREPARING HEART AND MIND

- Who do you find easier to trust — God or people? Why?

- In what areas of your life do you find it most difficult to trust God?

engaging the text

setting the stage

- The previous chapter (Hebrews 11) lists the Bible's "heroes of faith"—men and women who trusted God with all their hearts, even though some lost their lives. Hebrews 12 begins with the image of "a great cloud of witnesses," referring to these heroes of faith.

- Hebrews is written to people in the midst of persecution. The testimony of these witnesses would be a source of encouragement and comfort.

- The writer paints a picture of an athletics competition with witnesses cheering on the runners, thus encouraging them to do their best, to get up and go on even if they trip and fall, and to finish the race.

- The whole passage reflects support and reassurance for the runner, not fault-finding or criticism.

Read Hebrews 12:1–13

1. In verse 1, the "cloud of witnesses" refers to the men and women listed in the previous chapter (see Setting the Stage). Who models this kind of faith to you and so helps to "cheer you on" in your own walk of faith? Explain how they do that.

2. Verse 1 compares life with running a race. What kinds of things would an athlete not want with him when running a race? Explain why.

3. What hindrances might you still need to "throw off" in running your "race" of life? Keep in mind that these things may not be bad in themselves. Explain why or how they are hindrances to you personally.

4. The author also exhorts us to "run with perseverance." What helps you to persevere?

How would you know that you are persevering?

Know Your Grammar!

Trust is a verb for the noun faith.

5. Many of us find that our faith is too small to deal with the big issues in our lives. In what areas do you find that your faith may be too small?

6. Jesus is called the "author and perfecter" of our faith (v. 2). Think about what the writer means by this. What implications do these truths have for your answer to Question 5?

The Faithfulness of God

Many of us struggle over the feeling that we have too little faith. The great missionary pioneer into the inland of China, James Hudson Taylor, struggled as well. When he read the words of Mark 11:22, "Have faith in God," he was discouraged. He would gladly increase in his faith if he only knew how! One day when he was reading this passage in the original Greek, something new struck him. Reading "*Ekete pistin Theou*," meaning "to have (or hold) the faithfulness of God," he saw that *we* do not have to struggle to get faith in God in some way. We only have to count on *God's* faithfulness. This knowledge gave him new freedom to relax in God's constant faithfulness.

7. In verse 3, the writer exhorts the Hebrews to "consider Jesus." Why are they to do this? (See Setting the Stage.)

8. Think of a situation in your own life which is a challenge to you. How would your perspective change toward this situation if you were to "consider Jesus?" (See also the article "The Faithfulness of God.")

9. In verses 5–6, the author explains why we should not lose heart when the Lord rebukes us. How does this fit with your own concept and experience of love and discipline?

10. In verses 7–10, we are told to endure hardship. What is your response to this? Is hardship worth it? Explain.

Embracing and Enduring

"We also rejoice in our sufferings, because we know that suffering produces perseverance; perseverance, character; and character, hope" (Romans 5:3–4).

What does it mean to "rejoice in our sufferings?" It's not trying to avoid them or pretending they don't exist. It's not even gritting our teeth in quiet submission to our circumstances. It means to embrace every situation, however painful or disappointing it may be. God calls his people to rejoice, not in spite of tribulation, but *because* of it. To the world this response would seem insane. But it is the most reasonable thing we can do when we understand what immeasurable benefits tribulation brings to us.

There is no greater witness in the world than that of Christians who endure, who truly embrace God's will for their lives and thus overcome everything the world and the devil can throw at them. Making these things work for us and not against us is the key to real faith and real spiritual warfare.

Have there been difficult times in your life when you questioned God's love, wisdom, or power? How can you "consider it pure joy" (James 1:2) in the middle of difficult circumstances? How will this affect your behavior and thought life?

11. Think of a time when you were disciplined by God and you can now see the results of that discipline in your life. Would you prefer *not* to have been disciplined, or are you thankful you were, in spite of the pain? Explain why.

12. According to this passage, what is the connection between faith and suffering?

13. Think of issues or circumstances that tend to make you grow weary and lose heart (v. 3). How does this whole passage, with its emphasis on considering Jesus, help you to "strengthen your feeble arms and weak knees" and "make level paths for your feet" (vv. 12–13) (or, change your perspective and continue with endurance)?

Responding to God

Consider again the "hindrances" you thought of in Question 3. Ask God to help you "throw them off" and stay away from them.

Now think of your response to Question 13. Ask God to help you make use of the things that build your faith.

Thank God for providing Jesus as the one who, reflecting the Father, leads us and strengthens, sustains, and completes our faith.

> **Now faith is being sure of what we hope for and certain of what we do not see.**
>
> *Hebrews 11:1*

taking it further
Suggestions for application

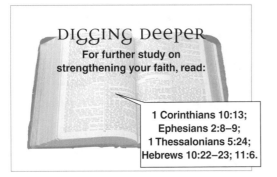

DIGGING DEEPER
For further study on strengthening your faith, read:

1 Corinthians 10:13;
Ephesians 2:8–9;
1 Thessalonians 5:24;
Hebrews 10:22–23; 11:6.

Personal Expression

Write a poem or a song expressing your commitment to "run with perseverance," accepting hardship as discipline from a loving Father. Keep in mind that Jesus is always there as the "author and perfecter of our faith," reflecting the support that the Father gives us. Ask God to speak to you as you write.

WORLD FOCUS

Read about Hudson Taylor on the next page. China is still a country with millions who do not know Christ and much persecution among those who do. Pray for:

- the Chinese who do not yet know Christ, that they will come to faith in the only true God.
- the Christians in China, that they will stay true to their God and their faith.
- the missionaries working among the Chinese.

"Prayer Strategies for Changing Nations" (on pages 102–4) could also be helpful.

Meditation

All too often we read over "little" words when we concentrate on the big picture of a Scripture passage. There are many statements in the Bible that are either connected, preceded, or followed by such words as "so that," "therefore," "for this reason," and "but." The meaning of a passage or sentence could change drastically if these words were not there. Several of these words are found in Hebrews 12:1–13. Identify them and meditate on the significance of each one. Note how your understanding of the passage is enriched as you do so.

PEOPLE OF IMPACT

HUDSON TAYLOR (1832–1905)
Perseverance and Faith

Conversation died the moment they spotted him. Some lowered their eyes in embarrassment, while others glared at him with contempt for his Chinese garb, shaved head, and pigtail. One thing was certain: Hudson Taylor's reappearance amongst the Europeans in Shanghai was not welcomed. Foreigners had grown wealthy on the lucrative trade in the bustling Chinese city. Hudson Taylor upset the established order of things. Even the other missionaries dismissed him without a second thought.

Yet a second thought was precisely what the Chinese were giving him. At first glance, most hardly noticed. It was his message, shouted above the din of the street, that turned their heads, demanding a second hearing. He had no wares to sell—just an old worn Book and a dynamic message of hope. Listening to him, it wasn't hard to believe that this Savior he spoke of had come just for them.

Born in Yorkshire, England, Hudson had already decided by the age of five that he would be a missionary to China. He prepared zealously for the difficult life he knew lay ahead, denying himself material comforts and devoting himself to prayer. His initial experiences in China convinced him of the need for new missionary strategies. So he founded the China Inland Mission in 1865 to provide an avenue for those without professional or academic qualifications to serve there. All he asked was that applicants lay down their lives for the Chinese, identify with them in lifestyle, and trust God to supply personal needs. Taylor's principles had a profound effect, and within fifty years of its inception, the China Inland Mission had become the largest foreign mission organization in the world. His principles for ministry and his teachings about the need for a deep experience of Jesus Christ came from the intense suffering of loneliness, rejection, and depression with which he struggled during his early years in China. Through it all, the testimony of his life of service can be captured in the profound words he once spoke: "God's work done in God's way will never lack God's supplies."

Responding to the Cross
Luke 23:32–49

session SIX

Barabbas would never be the same. Imagine him describing the day when he heard the crowd screaming, "Crucify him!" (Mark 15:6–15).

"I knew I deserved to die for my crimes," he might say. "But when soldiers shoved me out the prison door, they didn't take me to the cross; no, they set me free!

"How could this be? I strained for a glimpse of the lone figure standing before Pilate. No one could explain the crimes of this man Jesus who was to die in my place.

"Some people say that he was murdered for no reason at all. I don't really know, but one thing is sure: his death satisfied the authorities, and they let me live."

> **But he was pierced for our transgressions, he was crushed for our iniquities.**
>
> **— Isaiah 53:5**

There is no record of how Barabbas responded to Jesus taking his place, but the significance of his death on the cross cannot be ignored. We too were under the sentence of death, condemned by our sins. Jesus died in our place. By declaring faith in Jesus, we accept his death as an exchange of life—his for ours. In this study we will look at how Jesus reflects the heart of God the Father on the cross, and we will consider afresh our own response.

PREPARING HEART AND MIND

- What words come to your mind when you think of the cross?

- We see the cross everywhere. What do you think it means to people?

- How do you respond to the phrase, "Jesus died for you?"

SESSION SIX: Responding to the Cross

engaging the text

setting the stage

- According to Roman law of the time, no Roman citizen can be crucified. Crucifixion is reserved for non-Roman slaves and criminals.

- Thieves and robbers are considered criminals. Thieves steal secretly, while robbers steal openly and often violently. The Hebrew language does not differentiate between the two words, but the Greek does. Jesus is crucified between two robbers (Matthew 27:38; Mark 15:27; Luke 23:32).

- The Sanhedrin (the highest Jewish court) has no power to execute a death sentence; only the Roman government can do so.

- The Sanhedrin cannot find Jesus guilty of any charge. Even the charges of false witnesses collapse. Jesus himself gives them the evidence they want when he openly acknowledges that he is the Messiah, which to the Sanhedrin presents the charge of blasphemy (Matthew 26:59–66).

- The Roman government is also unable to find any charge against Jesus. Pilate condemns him to be crucified, knowing him to be innocent, simply to satisfy the crowd's demands (Matthew 27:23–26).

- According to God's perspective, Jesus *has* to be crucified! In Jewish law, God's curse is pronounced against someone dying in such a way (Deuteronomy 21:22–23). By enduring this particular form of death, Jesus absorbs in his own person the curse which the lawbreaker is under: "Christ redeemed us from the curse of the law by becoming a curse for us, for it is written: 'Cursed is everyone who is hung on a tree'" (Galatians 3:13).

Read Luke 23:32–49

1. In verse 34, Jesus asks the Father to forgive "them." Who do you think might be included in the term "them?" Explain why.

2. What does this response of Jesus tell you about him and how he reflects the Father's heart?

3. The fact that verse 34 is recorded in the Bible tells us that Jesus' words are heard by those watching. Imagine if you were a bystander and heard them. How might you respond?

SESSION SIX: Responding to the Cross

4. Identify the groups of people in verses 35–37 who are present at the crucifixion. What are their responses, and why do you think they respond that way?

The Horrors of Crucifixion

- Crucifixion was the most severe—and common—form of execution in the Roman Empire. It was aimed at humiliating and torturing the victim while intimidating the onlookers.
- Those sentenced to be crucified were usually beaten with leather lashes, which had sharp bits of bone and iron fastened on the ends. This often resulted in severe blood loss.
- The naked victim was then fastened to a cross with ropes or, in rare cases, nails through the wrists and feet. A block or peg was sometimes fastened to the stake as a crude seat.
- As the victim hung dangling by the arms, the blood could no longer circulate to the vital organs, and air could not reach the lungs. Only by supporting themselves on the "seat" could victims gain relief. Gradually exhaustion would set in, although death sometimes took several days. If victims had been severely beaten, they did not live this long.
- To hasten death, the executioners sometimes broke the victims' legs with a club. They could then no longer support their bodies to keep the blood circulating and to prevent suffocation. Death quickly followed.

5. In what ways do people today respond when they are confronted with the cross? How is it either similar to or different from how people responded 2000 years ago?

6. Although the two criminals are in the same situation and being justly punished, they respond very differently to Jesus (vv. 39–43). Why do you think they respond as they do, and what are the consequences?

7. Think of some occasions when you have shown similar responses to Jesus as these two criminals. How did Jesus reflect the Father's heart when he responded to you?

The Cross

The cross is impossible to overlook in the history of the human race. It refuses to be ignored. It demands a response!

8. Consider what the words *justice*, *grace*, and *mercy* mean to you. Which of these does the cross primarily represent to you? Explain why.

9. In verse 43, Jesus says, "Today you will be with me in paradise." Think about what he means and rephrase the sentence in your own words.

10. In verses 44–45, we receive a glimpse of how God the Father responds to his Son on the cross. Why do you think the Father responds in this way?

11. The centurion praises God when he sees what happens (v. 47). He has undoubtedly seen many crucifixions. Why do you think he responds in this way? (See also Matthew 27:50–54 and Mark 15:39 for other details.)

Forgiven for All Time

"Who is a God like you . . . ? You will again have compassion on us; you will tread our sins underfoot and hurl all our iniquities into the depths of the sea" (Micah 7:18–19).

As part of the celebration of the Jewish feast of Rosh Hashana, Esther and her family went to the top of the hill overlooking a deep lake. From there they threw small pebbles and larger rocks into the lake. As they disappeared into the watery depths, it was obvious they would never be found again. Those pebbles and rocks represent our sins—and what our heavenly Father does with them through his forgiveness.

Jesus paid the price for that forgiveness. His death on the cross means that no sin we have ever committed is too big that it can't be swallowed up by his forgiveness. He promises to tread our sins underfoot—and he has the biggest feet in the cosmos! Forgiveness is the cornerstone of relationship. Because our Father God wants a relationship with us, he is both willing and able to forgive us for any sin in our lives.

Is there some sin you've kept hidden, thinking God couldn't forgive you? Confess it to him today and watch it get swallowed up in his wondrous love!

12. Consider what Jesus is focused on in his dying moments, as recorded in this passage and also in John 19:26–27. What does this tell you about Jesus and how he reflects the Father's heart?

13. Jesus' death deals with *all* sin—including each of yours! He has paid for them on the cross, clearing you of all debt the moment you put your faith in him and ask for forgiveness. Through him, you are now righteous before the Father! How do you respond to a God like this?
    - This truth brings me great joy.
    - I can't quite grasp this truth.
    - I feel guilty when I hear that Jesus died for my sin.
    - I'm grateful.
    - Other (explain):

Responding to God

Thank Jesus for what he did for you. Ask him to help you grasp more fully what it cost him to present you holy before the Father.

> I have been crucified with Christ and I no longer live, but Christ lives in me.
>
> *Galatians 2:20*

taking it further
Suggestions for application

DIGGING DEEPER

For further study on the significance of the cross and our response to it, see:

1 Corinthians 1:18; Philippians 2:5–8; 3:17–18; Colossians 2:13b–14; Hebrews 12:1–2; 1 Peter 2:24.

Personal Expression

The symbol of the cross means different things to different people. Create your own cross as a symbol of what it has come to mean to you, in contrast to the very general meaning it often has today. You can build it, draw or paint it, make a collage—whatever materials you wish to use. Display your cross in a place where you will see it regularly and be reminded of what it signifies for you.

Connecting to Life

Read the article "Forgiven for All Time" and answer the question at the end: Is there some sin you've kept hidden, thinking God couldn't forgive you?

Confess it to him today and take hold of the truth that Christ has fully paid the price for your forgiveness. You may want to pray about it with a trusted friend, or do what Esther and her family did: take a stone to represent the sin and throw it into a river, lake, or the sea, to symbolize the fact that you are forgiven for all time!

Connecting to Life

Write down definitions of the words *grace* and *mercy* as you have come to understand them through this study. Identify a situation or relationship where you can invite God to help you extend that same grace and mercy that has been extended to you. Do what he prompts you to do.

Leader's Notes

Leading a Bible study—especially for the first time—can make you feel both nervous and excited. If you are nervous, realize that you are in good company. Many biblical leaders, such as Moses, Joshua, and the apostle Paul, felt nervous and inadequate to lead others (see, for example, 1 Corinthians 2:3). Yet God's grace was sufficient for them, just as it will be for you.

Some excitement is also natural. Your leadership is a gift to the others in the group. Keep in mind, however, that other group members also share responsibility for the group. Your role is simply to stimulate discussion by asking questions and encouraging people to respond. The suggestions below can help you to be an effective leader.

The Role of the Holy Spirit

Always remember that the work of the Holy Spirit is necessary in order for each of us to understand and apply God's Word. Prayer, your prayer for one another, is critical for revelation to take place. You can be assured that God is working in every group member's life. Look for what is stirring in people's hearts. Listen to their statements and questions, and be aware of what they do not say as well as what they do say. Watch God do his work. He will help you lead others and feed you at the same time. May God's blessing be with you.

Preparing to Lead

1. Ask God to help you understand and apply the passage to your own life. Unless this happens, you will not be prepared to lead others.
2. Carefully work through each question in the study guide. Meditate and reflect on the passage as you formulate your answers.

3. Familiarize yourself with the leader's notes for the session. These will help you understand the purpose of the session and will provide valuable information about the questions.
4. Pray for the various members of the group. Ask God to use these studies to help you grow as disciples of Jesus Christ.
5. Before each meeting, make sure each person has a study guide. Encourage them to prepare beforehand for each study.

Leading the Study

Opening (approximately 5 minutes)

1. At the beginning of your first time together, take a little extra time to explain that the Living Encounters are designed for discussions, sharing, and prayer together, not as lectures. Encourage everyone to participate, but realize that some may be hesitant to speak during the first few sessions.
2. Begin on time. If people realize that the study begins on schedule, they will work harder to arrive on time. Open in prayer. You may then want to ask for feedback from one person who has followed through on the "Taking It Further" section from the previous week's study.
3. Read the introduction together. This will orient the group to the passage being studied.

Preparing Heart and Mind (approximately 15 minutes)

1. Although these questions may be considered by individuals beforehand, you are strongly encouraged to begin your group time with them. They are designed to provoke thinking about a topic that is directly related to the study. Anyone who wrestles with one or more of the questions will be better prepared to receive the truth found in the rest of the study.

2. If your time is very limited, encourage your group members to consider one or more of the questions before they arrive. It is not necessary to mention them in your meeting. However, you may want to ask for one person who has already considered the questions to share thoughts about one question with the group before moving on to "Engaging the Text."

Engaging the Text (approximately 50 minutes)

1. This section is a study of one or more passages of Scripture. Read the Scripture portion(s) aloud. You may choose to do this yourself, or you might ask for volunteers.
2. There are normally 10–12 questions, which will take the group through an inductive process of looking at the text. These questions are designed to be used just as they are written. If you wish, you may simply read each one aloud. Or you may prefer to express a question in your own words until it is clearly understood. Unnecessary rewording, however, is not recommended.
3. Don't be afraid of silence. People in the group may need time to think before responding.
4. Avoid answering your own questions. Even an eager group will quickly become passive and silent if they think the leader will do most of the talking.
5. Encourage more than one answer to each question. Ask, "What do the rest of you think?" or "Anyone else?" until several people have had a chance to respond.
6. Try to be affirming whenever possible. Let people know you appreciate their insights into the passage.
7. Never reject an answer. If it is clearly wrong, ask, "Which verse led you to that conclusion?" Or let the group handle the problem by asking them what they think about the question.

8. Avoid going off on tangents. If people wander off course, gently bring them back to the passage being considered.
9. End on time. This will be easier if you control the pace of the discussion by not spending too much time on some questions or too little on others.

Articles

There are several articles in each study that are set off by gray boxes. These offer additional information as well as help to liven up the group time. "Setting the Stage" relates directly to the study of the passage, and questions will refer you to this sidebar when needed. Other gray-boxed articles can further illustrate or apply a principle. Become acquainted with the articles beforehand so that you know what is available. Remember that reading one or more of these articles in the group will add to your meeting time.

Responding to God (approximately 10 minutes)

In every study guide a prayer response is built into the last few minutes of the group time. This is to allow for the Holy Spirit to bring further revelation as well as application of the truths studied into each person's life. Usually there is a suggested way to respond in prayer, but feel free to adjust that as you sense what God is doing.

Taking It Further

You may want to encourage people to do one or more of these suggestions during the week ahead. Perhaps ask one person to share about it at your next time together. Or, depending on your time constraints, you may choose to do some of these activities during your session together.

Many more suggestions and helps are found in the book *Leading Bible Discussions* (InterVarsity Press). Reading it would be well worth your time.

SESSION ONE

Mirror Image of the Father
John 14:1–14

Purpose: For people to grow in their understanding that the Creator of heaven and earth, the almighty, eternal, infinite, unequaled, holy God is perfectly reflected in the person Jesus, who calls us his friends. Do you want to see what God is like? Look at Jesus—he is "the radiance of God's glory and the exact representation of his being" (Hebrews 1:3).

Engaging the Text

Question 1 These could be words like: distant, austere-looking, on a throne, judging, mystical, unapproachable, holy.

Question 2 These could be words like: warm, kind, caring, approachable, friendly, "human," understanding. For most people, there is a marked difference between the kind of words used in these two lists. The goal of these questions is to highlight the distorted concepts of God that people have and to create in them a desire to correct these views. As we look to Jesus and get to know him better, our views of the Father change too.

Question 3 Thirteen times, which is a significant number in just 14 verses. Give the group time to count how often the word appears—it helps to observe the text better—before moving on to the discussion. The aim is for participants to see more clearly the very definite and intimate connection Jesus draws between the Father and himself.

Question 4 There are six parallels, one being repeated, in verses 1b, 6b, 7, 9b, 10a, 10c, and 11a. There could be slight differences of opinion in the group, which is fine. The point is not what is right and wrong, but rather, to work with the text and learn from it. Participants are recognizing that Jesus makes many statements about his oneness with the Father.

Question 5 It may be appropriate to add to the discussion by asking the question: "The disciples know Jesus well; they have been with him for about three years. If the Father and Jesus are one, how would grasping that help their view of God?" The inaccessible God of their understanding has suddenly become accessible through their good friend Jesus. God is accessible, knowable, trustworthy, visible, and touchable in Jesus.

Question 7 Jesus is responding with immense understanding for where the disciples are, with patience, love, and gentleness. The one who is about to suffer and be sacrificed continues to take the role of comforter.

Question 8 Jesus and Thomas are talking on two different levels. Jesus is speaking of a spiritual reality—his Father's house (the Greek word, *oikia*, is used, meaning a residence or place where one dwells, which therefore refers to where God dwells, which is heaven). Thomas, however, is thinking of a geographical location somewhere in this world, and how can he know how to get there? Thomas has still not grasped the fullness of who Jesus, the Messiah, really is, or his goal. Neither have any of the other disciples, as is evident in their question recorded in Acts 1:6: "Lord, are you at this time going to restore the kingdom to Israel?"

Question 9 Jesus is saying something about *who he is* (his nature), and *what he is like* (his character). Have the group identify these things, for example, "*I am* the way."

Question 11 Thomas wants a "map" to where Jesus is going. Jesus says to him, "*I am* your map!" Philip wants to see the Father. Jesus says to him, "Look at *me!* You *are* seeing the Father!" The fact that group members would share this experience implies that they have also realized their error and corrected it. Give freedom for them to share this as well if they wish to.

Responding to God

It may be appropriate to divide the group into twos and threes and encourage people to pray for each other concerning these issues.

Taking It Further

Refer to the explanation of this section in the introduction to the Leader's Notes. While not a requirement, the aim of these suggestions is to help the study have a continuing effect on people's lives through the following week. Encourage people to choose one or more of the activities which appeal to them. Make it clear that they are not expected to follow through on all the suggestions.

session two

tHe One Who Understands
Hebrews 4:12–5:4

Purpose: To help participants better grasp that Jesus is our sympathetic "high priest" who understands our weaknesses and is able to help us.

Engaging the Text

Question 1 While there might be more than one answer to this question, the aim is for participants to recognize that nothing is hidden from God—his Word and Spirit uncover the deepest secrets of our heart.

There is no "right" answer here. The aim is to help people be honest with how they feel. Although some may feel perfectly at ease, others will feel rather vulnerable, maybe wanting to hide.

Question 3 It might not be appropriate to have the group share the first part of this question. However, encourage discussion around their responses to the second part, even if group members don't share details.

Question 5 Criteria for high priest: he is selected from among men (v. 1), he is appointed (v. 1), he is called by God, like Aaron (v. 4). Function of high priest: To represent people to God (v. 1), to offer gifts and sacrifices for sins (v. 1), to offer sacrifices for his own sins as well as for the people (v. 3). Abilities of high priest: To be able to deal gently with people, since he himself is subject to weakness (v. 2).

Question 6 Jesus fits completely, except that he is without sin and therefore does not offer sacrifices for his own sins.

session three

following in the footsteps of forgiveness
Luke 7:36–50

Purpose: To show that Jesus' forgiveness reflects God's heart of forgiveness toward us, and that he enables us to forgive one another.

Engaging the Text

Question 1 Simon could not have forgotten to show these signs of hospitality to Jesus. Not doing so shows the utmost disrespect, like a slap in the face. You might like to bring up the question, "What about the other guests? Did Simon show them these signs of hospitality?" Have people check the text, although it doesn't give an answer. You can then point the attention to what we *do* know, which is the information given in "Setting the Stage." It seems very unlikely that Simon, a religious leader in the community, would *not* show these signs of hospitality to his other guests, which makes his failure with Jesus even more of an insult.

Question 4 Jesus was probably hurt and also perhaps grieved over Simon's hardness of heart.

Although the text does not say anything directly, the lack of any evidence of Jesus "getting back" at Simon speaks for itself. He merely reclines at the table and eats. The aim here is to help participants think about their own responses when people treat them ungraciously or unjustly.

Question 5   Simon's heart is clearly more important to Jesus than Simon's actions, however much Jesus himself is affected by his ungraciousness. He waits for an opportune moment to deal with Simon's hard heart, and he does it for Simon's sake, not his own. It is more important to Jesus to help Simon see his hard heart, possibly affecting Simon for the rest of his life, than to expose an ungracious act that affects Jesus on a single occasion.

Question 6   There is no right or wrong answer here. The goal is to discuss possibilities, given the facts we have, of what goes on in Simon's head and heart. Some possible answers:

- Simon only hears words of rebuke. Whether his deceit and self-importance allow him to understand how Jesus' parable applies to himself is hard to say, but he most certainly understands the reprimand after the story. With what reaction?

- Shame.

- Anger at Jesus for humiliating him before the woman and his guests.

- Indignation at Jesus for daring to suggest that this woman's sins can be forgiven, and even more so that Jesus is the one who is extending forgiveness, as if he is God.

Although the text does not say, it is fairly safe to assume that the woman hears only words of compassion, acceptance, and forgiveness. A new world and a new life probably open up to her. Her feelings could be such things as intense relief, thankfulness, a sense of freedom.

Question 7   Encourage the group to come up with some possibilities. These could be:

- He who has little need to be forgiven does not have much love;
- He who has not yet discovered (for whatever reason) how much he needs to be forgiven has not yet asked for forgiveness and therefore does not love the one extending forgiveness.

Always look at the details in the light of the whole context of the passage.

Responding to God

Forgiving could be a very sensitive issue for some participants, especially those with deep hurts. It may be appropriate to pray with some at another time or encourage them to pray further with a trusted friend. The sidebar "A Time for Restoration" could be helpful.

session four

Jesus Our Reconciler
Ephesians 2:11–18

Purpose: To help participants grasp that Jesus is the source of all true peace and reconciliation, both within ourselves and in all circumstances.

Engaging the Text

Question 1   To encourage the discussion you could add the following questions: Is true peace dependent on external or internal circumstances? Why?

Question 2   "You" were once uncircumcised, separate from Christ, excluded from Israel, foreigners to covenants, without hope, without God, far away. For "They," nothing is specified in verses 12–16, but the opposite of what is mentioned for "You" is implied.

Paul gives much more information about the Gentiles than the Jews because he is addressing the Gentiles. However, it is clear that he is contrasting the two groups. The purpose of this question is to help participants see the contrast (and separation) between the two, as this will form a platform for the next few questions.

Question 3   Some external barriers can be such things as doctrine, culture, language, and color. Internal barriers can be such things as misunderstanding, judgment, fear, stubbornness, unforgiveness, and pride. In mentioning the "dividing wall," Paul is also almost certainly referring to the physical wall in the temple which separates the outer court of the Gentiles from the court of the

Jews. This wall was a tangible reminder of the separation between Jews and Gentiles. Paul physically experiences the hostility caused by this very wall when he is innocently accused by the Jews of bringing a Gentile past that wall. He is subsequently attacked and almost killed by his fellow countrymen. (See Acts 21:27–36.)

Question 5   This question intentionally allows for group members either to be very personal in their sharing or remain more general if they choose.

Question 7   What is important is the tense of the verb. He *is* our peace, not *will be* or *will one day become* or even *is perhaps*. It is an established fact. In looking at the significance of the pronoun "our," the aim is to help people realize that the statement is made very personal. It also refers to *us*, to *me*.

Question 12 You may want to help the discussion by asking questions like: Could Jesus have "preached" peace without using words? How? You could also refer to the sidebar "A Definition of Peace."

session five

On to the finish Line with Jesus
Hebrews 12:1–13

Purpose: To enable participants to see that Jesus is the giver, the sustainer, and the perfecter of our faith. He enables us to persevere to the end with him.

Engaging the Text

Question 1   The aim here is to help people see that they are not in this "race" alone and that there are others from whom they receive help and encouragement.

Question 2   Most people have at some point run a real race—even if it was only in preschool! You could ask the group to think of such a time. What did it feel like? Remind them of the strain of the muscles, the breathlessness, especially if they didn't train. If any group members have been involved in long-distance running, ask them to share their understanding of the necessity of having as few hindrances as possible.

Question 3   It is important for people to grasp that possible hindrances are not inherently bad things in themselves. It is also important to recognize that what may be a hindrance for one person is not for another.

Question 4   There is no "right" answer to these questions. They simply stimulate thought about perseverance in the process of discussion.

Question 6 Encourage the group to discuss the writer's meaning first, without helps. After they have done so, you could have them check verse 2 in other available translations.

Question 7 The readers are facing persecution and hardship. Knowing that Jesus also experienced severe persecution and therefore understands what they are going through would be a tremendous comfort to them.

Question 8 Not everybody goes through persecution, but we all face various hardships and challenges. It can be life-changing for people to realize that it is not only in the "big" situations that Jesus can make a difference, but also in the "small" ones. The aim here is to help participants grasp this truth and the fact that Jesus is the one who gives faith in all circumstances and sustains it. He remains faithful, even when our own measure of faith is low.

Question 9 Many people see both discipline and punishment in a negative light, and it is true that discipline without love is no more than punishment. It is vital to understand, therefore, that when God our loving Father disciplines us, he does it out of unconditional love — not because he's mad at us, but because he wants us to be better children and to mature well. For some group members, their experience of rebuke, discipline, and punishment in their own family situation may have been less than godly. Encourage them to ask God to change their perception of his discipline and to help them see the truth.

Question 10 Again, it is significant for people to realize that the discipline of our loving heavenly Father is for our growth, in order that we might share in his holiness. It is during times of hardship, suffering, discipline, and correction that we can grow in holiness and righteousness and learn to see more clearly the Jesus whom we are following.

SESSION SIX

Responding to the Cross
Luke 23:32–49

Purpose: To recognize that the cross of Jesus Christ is an integral part of our faith and requires a response from us.

Engaging the Text

Question 1 In the immediate context, the term would refer to the soldiers who crucify Jesus, the Roman government who condemns him, and the Jewish leaders who want him killed. His disciples who desert him could possibly be included. Is there anybody else? Encourage people to express what they think.

Question 2 Some examples: his compassion for sinners, his unselfishness, his unconditional love, his understanding of the bigger picture (that is, Jesus understands his mission).

Question 4 *The people* (those who love him; those who are indifferent) stand watching. Possible reasons could be: they are interested, curious, compassionate.

The rulers (at least those who hate him) sneer. Possible reasons: their hatred; they are delighted to see him die.

The soldiers (those who are ignorant) mock him. Possible reasons: they see him as a common criminal, perhaps a madman.

Question 6 The first criminal is probably picking up on the sneering and mocking of the rulers and soldiers. Possible further reasons: unbelief or ignorance concerning who Jesus is; anger at his own situation; fear; the physical pain he is suffering. All culminates in a hard heart. The consequence: he is unable to enter the kingdom of heaven because of his hardness of heart.

The second criminal defends Jesus and in his own way asks for mercy. Possible reasons: a softened and repentant heart, even though he is suffering physically as much as the first criminal. The consequence: he enters the kingdom.

Question 8 There is no "right" answer to this question, the goal being to hear one another's views while staying in line with what the Scripture teaches. Help participants to avoid vague ideas and keep the discussion personal. How do the words relate to them personally? It may be appropriate to mention some possible definitions, below:

- Grace is receiving what we do not deserve.
- Mercy is not receiving what we do deserve.
- Justice is receiving what we deserve.

Question 9 Examples of rephrasing: "You are forgiven; I am giving you eternal life;" "As of today you will experience eternal life."

Question 10 As his Son becomes sin incarnate (see 2 Corinthians 5:21), it is impossible for a holy God to look at him. God hates sin. The curtain torn in two happens at the crucial moment when Jesus dies. (In this passage it may seem that it occurs before Jesus dies and might then be seen as the Father's response to sin. But the reports of the same situation found in Matthew 27:50–51 and Mark 15:37–38 clarify the timing.)

Question 11 It may be appropriate to have the group read the references in Matthew and Mark, as they give further details. The centurion's response must be due to more than simply seeing Jesus die.

There are no right or wrong answers, but it is the unusual circumstances that probably make the difference, such as the earthquake, the darkness, and Jesus' words while hanging on the cross.

Question 12 Jesus focuses on people: "Father, forgive them," he responds to the criminal; he sees that his mother is taken care of. This focus points us again to the nature and character of Jesus, which is the same as the Father's: his unselfishness, passion to forgive, concern for others. You could also draw from the group members which of these responses or words of Jesus touch them the most and why.

Hearing the Voice of God

If you know the Lord, you have already heard his voice—it is that inner leading that brought you to him in the first place. Jesus always checked with his Father (John 8:26–29), and so should we; hearing the voice of the heavenly Father is a basic right of every child of God. The following are a number of ways of fine-tuning this experience:

1. Hearing God's voice is possible for you!

Don't make guidance complicated. It's actually hard not to hear God if you really want to please and obey him! If you stay humble, he promises to guide you (Proverbs 16:9). Here are three simple steps to help in hearing his voice:

- *Submit* to his lordship. Ask him to help you silence your own thoughts and desires and the opinions of others that may be filling your mind (2 Corinthians 10:5). Even though you have been given a good mind to use, right now you want to hear the thoughts of the Lord, who has the *best* mind (Proverbs 3:5–6).
- *Resist* the enemy, in case he is trying to deceive you at this moment. Use the authority that Jesus Christ has given you to silence the voice of the enemy (Ephesians 6:10–20; James 4:7).
- *Expect* your loving heavenly Father to speak to you. After asking your question, wait for him to answer. He will (Exodus 33:11; Psalm 69:13; John 10:27).

2. God speaks in different ways

Allow God to speak to you in the way he chooses. Don't try to dictate to him concerning the guidance methods you prefer. He is Lord—you are his servant (1 Samuel 3:9). So listen with a yielded heart; there is a direct link between yieldedness and hearing. He may choose to speak to you through *his Word*. This could come in your daily reading of the Bible, or he could guide you to a particular verse (Psalm 119:105). He may speak to you through an *audible voice* (Exodus 3:4), through dreams (Matthew 2), or through *visions* (Isaiah 6:1; Revelation 1:12–17). But probably the most common way is through the quiet *inner voice* (Isaiah 30:21).

3	**Acknowledge your sin before God**	Confess any sin. A clean heart is necessary if you want to hear God (Psalm 66:18).
4	**Revisit the scene of God's guidance**	Use the Axhead Principle (see 2 Kings 6). If you seem to have lost your way, go back to the last time you knew the sharp, cutting edge of God's voice. Then obey. The key question is, "Have you obeyed the last thing God has told you to do?"
5	**God can and will speak to you!**	Get your own leading. God will use others to confirm your guidance, but you should also hear from him directly. It can be dangerous to rely on others to get the word of the Lord for you (1 Kings 13).
6	**God will make it clear in his time**	Don't talk about your guidance until God gives you permission to do so. Sometimes this happens immediately; at other times there is a delay. The main purpose of waiting is to avoid four pitfalls: *pride*—because God has spoken to you; *presumption*—by speaking before you have full understanding; *missing God's timing and method*; and *bringing confusion to others*, who also need prepared hearts (Ecclesiastes 3:7; Mark 5:19; Luke 9:36).
7	**Be alert to the signs God provides**	Use the Wise-Men Principle (see Matthew 2). Just as the wise men individually followed the star and were all led to the same Christ, so God will often use two or more spiritually sensitive people to *confirm* what he is telling you (2 Corinthians 13:1).
8	**Discern true guidance from false guidance**	Beware of counterfeits. Of course you have heard of a counterfeit dollar bill. But have you ever heard of a counterfeit paper bag? No. Why not? Because only things of value are worth counterfeiting. Satan has a counterfeit of everything of God that is possible for him to copy (Exodus 7:22; Acts 8:9–11). Counterfeit guidance comes, for example, through Ouija boards, seances, fortune-telling, and astrology (Leviticus 19:26; 20:6; 2 Kings 21:6). The guidance of the Holy Spirit leads you closer to Jesus and into true freedom. Satan's guidance leads you away from God into bondage. One key test for true guidance: Does your leading follow biblical principles? The Holy Spirit never contradicts the Word of God. Confess any sin. A clean heart is necessary if you want to hear God (Psalm 66:18).

9. Yield your heart completely to the Lord

Opposition from humans is sometimes guidance from God (Acts 21:10–14). The important thing again is yieldedness to the Lord (Daniel 6:6–23; Acts 4:18–21). Rebellion is never of God, but sometimes he asks us to step away from our elders in a way that is not rebellion but part of his plan. Trust that he will show your heart the difference.

10. God will reveal your calling

Every follower of Jesus has a unique ministry (Romans 12; 1 Corinthians 12; Ephesians 4:11–13; 1 Peter 4:10–11). The more you seek to hear God's voice in detail, the more effective you will be in your own calling. Guidance is not a game—it is serious business where we learn *what* God wants us to do and *how* he wants us to do it. The will of God is doing and saying the right thing in the right place, with the right people at the right time and in the right sequence, under the right leadership, using the right method with the right attitude of heart.

11. Stay in constant communication with God

Practice hearing God's voice and it becomes easier. It's like picking up the phone and recognizing the voice of your best friend... you know that voice because you have heard it so many times before. Compare the young Samuel with the older man Samuel (1 Samuel 3:4–7; 8:7–10; 12:11–18).

12. God wants a relationship with you!

Relationship is the most important reason for hearing the voice of the Lord. God is not only infinite, but personal. If you don't have communication, you don't have a personal relationship with him. True guidance is getting closer to the Guide. We grow to know the Lord better as he speaks to us; as we listen to him and obey him, we make his heart glad (Exodus 33:11; Matthew 7:24–27).

Loren Cunningham © 1984

Principles for Effective Intercession

1. Praise God for who he is, and for the privilege of engaging in the same wonderful ministry as the Lord Jesus (Hebrews 7:25). Praise God for the privilege of cooperating with him in the affairs of humankind through prayer.

2. Make sure your heart is clean before God by having given the Holy Spirit time to convict, should there be any unconfessed sin (Psalm 66:18; 139:23–24).

3. Acknowledge that you can't really pray without the direction and energy of the Holy Spirit (Romans 8:26). Ask God to utterly control you by his Spirit, receive by faith the reality that he does, and thank him (Ephesians 5:18).

4. Deal aggressively with the enemy. Come against him in the all-powerful name of the Lord Jesus Christ and with the "sword of the Spirit"—the Word of God (Ephesians 6:17; James 4:7).

5. Die to your own imaginations, desires, and burdens for what you feel you should pray about (Proverbs 3:5–6; 28:26; Isaiah 55:8).

6. Praise God now in faith for the remarkable prayer meeting you're going to have. He's a remarkable God, and he will do something consistent with his character.

7. Wait before God in silent expectancy, listening for his direction (Psalm 62:5; 81:11–13; Micah 7:7).

8. In obedience and faith, utter what God brings to your mind, believing (John 10:27). Keep asking God for direction, expecting him to give it to you. He will (Psalm 32:8). Make sure you don't move to the next subject until you've given God time to discharge all he wants to say regarding this burden—especially when praying in a group. Be encouraged by the lives of Moses, Daniel, Paul, and Anna, knowing that God gives revelation to those who make intercession a way of life.

9   If possible, have your Bible with you should God want to give you direction or confirmation from it (Psalm 119:105).

10   When God ceases to bring things to your mind for which to pray, finish by praising and thanking him for what he has done, reminding yourself of Romans 11:36: "For from him and through him and to him are all things. To him be the glory forever! Amen."

A WARNING: God knows the weakness of the human heart toward pride. If we speak of what God has revealed and done in intercession, it may lead to committing this sin. God shares his secrets with those who are able to keep them. There may come a time when he definitely prompts us to share, but unless this happens, we should remain silent: "The disciples kept this to themselves, and told no one at that time what they had seen" (Luke 9:36). "Mary treasured up all these things and pondered them in her heart" (Luke 2:19).

Joy Dawson © 1985

Prayer Strategies for Changing Nations

We all have an opportunity to affect the course of history. If we pray with clean hearts, regularly and effectively, for the nations, we become history shapers. We are to pray for all nations and to focus primarily on the body of Christ, the church, as God intends her to shape the course of history. This ministry of intercession also prepares her for future authority in his eternal kingdom (2 Chronicles 7:14; Job 12:23; Psalm 2:8–9; Isaiah 56:7; Daniel 7:27; Revelation 2:26–29).

Here are twelve steps to help you pray more effectively.

1 Thank and praise God for who he is and for:
- The privilege of cooperating with him in prayer.
- His involvement already in the nation for which he is leading you to pray (Philemon 4–6).

2 Pray for an unprecedented outpouring of the Holy Spirit upon the church worldwide (Psalm 85:6; Isaiah 64:1–3):
- That God's people would see that there is no substitute for revival, pray persistently, and be prepared for it. Consider these biblical promises for revival: Psalm 102:15–16; Isaiah 41:17–20; 45:8; 52:10; 59:19; 61:11; Hosea 6:3b; Zechariah 10:1.
- That the church would receive revelation of God's awesome holiness and unfathomable love leading to deep repentance, especially of the sins of idolatry, apathy, and disobedience, resulting in a passionate love for the Lord.

3 Pray for unity in the Body of Christ:
- For revelation of the pride and prejudice that separates.
- That reconciliation would result; success depends on it (Matthew 12:25).
- That seeing their need for each other, they would honor and prefer one another.
- That their manifest unity would influence the lost to come to Jesus Christ (John 17:23).

4   Pray for leaders (Judges 5:2; Psalm 75:7; Proverbs 8:13–15; 29:18; Ephesians 4:11):
- For spiritual leaders to be raised up who understand the character and ways of God and fear him.
- To receive vision related to the extension of God's kingdom worldwide.
- For righteous leaders to be placed into all spheres of authority and influence (Proverbs 28:2).
- That God would convict unrighteous leaders, and if they persist in sin, overthrow them.

5   Pray that God's Word would have its rightful place:
- As the basis for laws, moral values, and behavior (Psalm 119:126).
- That preachers and teachers would get their messages from God's Word, and live them and teach them (Jeremiah 23:22; 1 Corinthians 4:16–17).

6   Pray that God's people would see that obedience is the key to the Christian life, that God's priorities would become theirs (Psalm 19:11–14; 34:1; Proverbs 8:13; Matthew 4:10, 19; 2 Corinthians 7:1):
- A life of worship, praise, and intercession.
- Time alone with God, getting to know him through his Word, and waiting on him for directions.
- Having a heart burdened for the lost and witnessing to them.
- A biblical understanding and practice of the fear of the Lord that would permeate every believer's life.
- Fulfilling the conditions to be empowered by the Holy Spirit (Ephesians 5:18).

7   Pray for children and youth:
- To have the chance to be born, hear the gospel, and know that God loves them—that deliverance and healing would come to the abused and neglected.
- That God would raise up anointed ministries to teach them the character and ways of God.
- For revival to come among them.

8 Pray for workers:
- To be sent to every nation and from every nation (Matthew 9:38; 28:19–20).
- That every believer would embrace the mandate "Go to the nations," and seek the necessary grace to stay home if God so directs.

9 Pray for an increased effectiveness of the varied media ministries targeted to reach the lost.

10 Engage in spiritual warfare (Matthew 16:18):
- Against satanic attacks on both the church and the unsaved.
- Ask God to reveal principalities dominating nations and cities. Pray against them (Ephesians 6:12–13; James 4:7; Revelation 12:11).

11 Pray for spiritual awakening of the unconverted, motivating them to seek God:
- Salvation of unrighteous leaders.
- Radical conversions of most unlikely people, resulting in powerful ministries.
- Revelation to come to the ignorant and the deceived of Jesus' deity and claims, with resultant conversions.

12 Release faith:
- That your prayers are being answered (John 14:13; 16:24; 2 Peter 3:9)!
- That the nations will fear him. Praise God that he will rebuild his church and appear in his glory (Psalm 102:15–16).

Joy Dawson © 1990

World Map

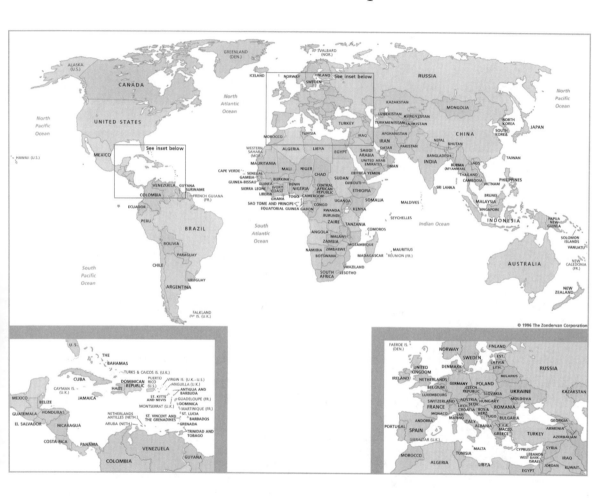

stay connected!

Living Encounters Series
Youth With A Mission

Styled after Youth With A Mission's (YWAM) successful Discipleship Training School (DTS), the Living Encounters series draws on YWAM's years of experience and expertise in training people of all ages for international ministry. Its unique, life-changing approach to Bible study will expand your small group's paradigm of Christianity ... liberate its spiritual passion ... and fill it with the joy and spiritual vigor that come from following an unpredictable, radical, and totally amazing risen Lord.

Experiencing the Spirit: *Living in the Active Presence of God*   0-310-22706-2
Seeing Jesus: *The Father Made Visible*   0-310-22707-0
Encountering God: *The God You've Always Wanted to Know*   0-310-22708-9
Building Relationships: *Connections for Life*   0-310-22709-7
Embracing God's Grace: *Strength to Face Life's Challenges*   0-310-22229-X
Expanding Your View: *Seeing the World God's Way*   0-310-22704-6
Making God Known: *Offering the Gift of Life*   0-310-22703-8
Finding Your Purpose: *Becoming All You Were Meant to Be*   0-310-22702-X

Look for Living Encounters at your local Christian bookstore.
ZondervanPublishingHouse

About Youth With A Mission

The Heart of Youth With A Mission

Youth With A Mission (YWAM) is an international movement of Christians from many denominations dedicated to presenting Jesus Christ personally to this generation, to mobilizing as many as possible to help in this task, and to training and equipping believers for their part in fulfilling the Great Commission. As Christians of God's Kingdom, we are called to love, worship, and obey our Lord, to love and serve his body, the Church, and to present the whole gospel for the whole man throughout the whole world.

We in Youth With A Mission believe that the Bible is God's inspired and authoritative Word, revealing that Jesus Christ is God's Son; that man is created in God's image; and that he created us to have eternal life through Jesus Christ; that although all men have sinned and come short of God's glory, God has made salvation possible through the death on the cross and resurrection of Jesus Christ.

We believe that repentance, faith, love, and obedience are fitting responses to God's initiative of grace toward us; that God desires all men to be saved and to come to the knowledge of truth; and that the Holy Spirit's power is demonstrated in and through us for the accomplishing of Christ's last commandment: "Go into all the world and preach the good news to all creation" (Mark 16:15).

How Youth With A Mission Works

YWAM embraces three modes of action—ways which we believe God has given us to be a part of the goal of taking the gospel to all the world:

Evangelism — spreading God's message.
Training — preparing workers to reach others.
Mercy Ministries — showing God's love through practical assistance.

Youth With A Mission has a particular mandate for mobilizing and championing the ministry potential of young people. But our worldwide missions force also includes thousands of older people from all kinds of social, cultural, ethnic, and professional backgrounds. Our staff of 12,000 includes people from more than 135 nations and ranges from relatively new Christians to veteran pastors and missionaries.

We are committed to a lifestyle of dependence on God for guidance, financial provision, and holy living. We also affirm a lifestyle of worship, prayer, godly character, hospitality, generosity, servant leadership, team ministry, personal responsibility, and right relationships with one another and our families.

Because of its visionary calling, YWAM does new things in new ways where new initiatives are required. We seek to build bridges among Christian leaders, partnering with local churches and missions for completion of the Great Commission. Annually, over 35,000 people from various churches take part in YWAM's short-term outreach projects.

Teams from Youth With A Mission have now ministered in every country of the world and have ministry centers in 142 nations, but the work is far from complete. We welcome all who want to know God and make him known to join with us in finishing the task — to "make disciples of all nations" (Matthew 28:19).

for more information

For more information about YWAM, please contact YWAM Publishing to obtain YWAM's *Go Manual*, an annual directory of YWAM's addresses and training and service opportunities (send $5 to cover costs), or write one of our field offices for more information. Note: Please mention the Living Encounters Bible study series in your request for information.

YWAM Field Offices

Youth With A Mission
(The Americas Office)
P.O. Box 4600
Tyler, TX 75712 U.S.A.
1-903-882-5591

Youth With A Mission
(Europe, Middle East, & Africa Office)
Highfield Oval, Harpenden
Herts. AL5 4BX
England, U.K.
(44) 1582-463-300

Youth With A Mission
(Pacific & Asia Office)
P.O. Box 7
Mitchell, A.C.T. 2911
Australia
(61) 6-241-5500

YWAM International DTS
(Discipleship Training School) Centre
PF 608
Budapest 62
1399 Hungary
100726.1773@compuserve.com

YWAM Publishing

P.O. Box 55787
Seattle, WA 98155 U.S.A.
Phone: 1-800-922-2143 (U.S. only) or
1-425-771-1153
Fax: 1-425-775-2383
E-mail address:
75701.2772@compuserve.com
Web page:
www.ywampublishing.com

DISCOVER YOUR PERSONAL PATH TOWARD INTIMACY WITH GOD

CHRISTIAN GROWTH STUDY BIBLE
New International Version

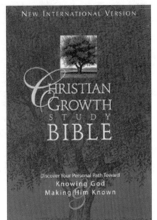

If you've enjoyed this YWAM study guide, you'll love this YWAM study Bible! The *Christian Growth Study Bible* is designed to help you cultivate heart-to-heart closeness with God. The kind you've longed for and God created you for. A dynamic, growing relationship so vital and life-changing that you can't keep it to yourself—you've got to tell the world about it and help others discover the greatness of your heavenly Father.

Knowing God and Making Him Known is the heartbeat of the *Christian Growth Study Bible*. It's also the heartbeat of Youth With A Mission (YWAM). Which is why this Bible's study program is modeled after YWAM's proven approach in their Discipleship Training Schools. At last, here's a study Bible with a 30-path program that will help you take the uncertainty out of your Christian growth. It helps you determine where you are on the path toward maturity—and helps remove the guesswork about where to go from there.

This *Christian Growth Study Bible* will be an invaluable tool for you to use with your Living Encounters Bible study series, giving you further help on the topics you will be exploring.

Hardcover	ISBN 0-310-91809X	
	ISBN 0-310-918138 Indexed	
Softcover	ISBN 0-310-918103	
Black Bonded Leather	ISBN 0-310-91812X	
	ISBN 0-310-918154 Indexed	
Burgundy Bonded Leather	ISBN 0-310-918111	
	ISBN 0-310-918146 Indexed	

We want to hear from you. Please send your comments about this book to us in care of the address below. Thank you.

ZondervanPublishingHouse
Grand Rapids, Michigan 49530
http://www.zondervan.com